# LET ME TELL YOU WHAT I KNOW

### ANN-GELA HOLLOWAY

ANN GELA
HOLLOWAY
CONSULTING

HK

Estd. 1995

**Book Creation & Design**
DHBonner Virtual Solutions
www.dhbonner.net

ISBN 978-0-578-80595-5

Printed in the United States of America

# DEDICATION

First, I would like to dedicate this book to the memory of my brother, *Willie Holloway, Jr.*, who passed away in 2003 at the age of thirty-four with many manuscripts left unwritten. I did it, big bro! I wrote a book!

I'll never forget that one summer when you wrote and directed an entire episode of "Gimme a Break" for us to act out. It was my first time performing in a role. I am not sure if that was my first exposure to storytelling, but it stands as a defining moment in my life. Thank you, also, for the five-hundred dollars you gave me when Social Security finally approved your disability status. I have never had someone give me that much money and not want to be repaid or expect anything in return.

That was your heart! And that is why you didn't survive your transplant surgery . . . because just any old heart would never do! Most transplant recipients reject their new heart, but your new heart rejected you because it could have never filled the void left by your old one. I love you, Willie. Until we meet again...

To my parents, *Willie and Joann Holloway*, thanks for giving me life! I once read that anyone born in the 1970s, after the legalization of abortion and the wide availability of birth control, is truly a miracle!

To my sons, *Andre and Alexander* — You two guys are the reasons behind most of what I do! Andre, your birth led me to salvation in Jesus Christ. Something about your being born made me want to raise you in church. I had no clue what I was looking for when I first stepped into the church, but I am glad to say that I found it. Alexander, by the time you came into my life, I realized all of the things that I had taken for granted, including time! Thanks for being the push that I needed in this second half of my life.

# TABLE OF CONTENTS

# INTRODUCTION

This book is about what I know. It is not about what I don't know. It's about what I've experienced and what I've learned from those experiences. This book is about my walk with God. And because my journey through life continues, there will be new experiences and new learnings along the way!

I needed to state that — I needed to make that declaration. You see, one of the things that kept this book from being written was my apprehension with my level of knowledge on these subjects. I questioned how qualified I was to write this book. I wondered if anyone would want to read it or hear anything I had to say. I thought my words would be challenged, researched, and even debunked.

Hmm . . . challenged, researched, and debunked?

Did I really have apprehension with my level of knowledge on these subjects? So, I actually questioned how qualified I was to write this?

Wait a minute! How does one question *their* ability to share *their* experiences? Basically, I told myself that I couldn't write about my truth. What a lie that was!

If I still walked while carrying embarrassment and shame (which, thankfully, I do not), I would have been embarrassed by those thoughts. However, since I am walking in newfound freedom, you are now holding my book in your hands! And believe me, that opening statement of declaration was reread and referred to often as I was completing this book.

> "Then you will experience for yourselves the truth, and the truth will free you."
>
> —John 8:32 MSG

This book is about my truth; being afraid to write about my truth was a symptom of a much bigger problem. The problem is that most people do not know their truth! They don't know what they believe or what they stand for. They can't emphatically say what holds true in their lives. We walk around like this most days, until someone calls us out about it.

For me, it was at a women's conference when one of the speakers encouraged us to find our inner truth. What is it that you know? How did you learn it? And are you willing to share that with someone else? My answer to the latter question is 'Yes'. My answers to the former questions are written out in the pages that follow!

I know what I know; and what I don't know will be in the next book! So, for now, let's talk about what I do know!

# GRACE FOR
# THE MOMENT

> "GOD is our refuge and strength, always ready
> to help in times of trouble."
>
> —Psalms 46:1 NLT

One of the concepts that I am most excited to share is the revelation of grace for the moment. If you've ever dealt with fear, anxiety, or worry, you need to know about grace for the moment. The best way that I describe it is that when you need it, it will be there. The "it" will vary from person-to-person and situation-to-situation. The "it" shows up when you need it. Often, the "it" gets there first, right on time to help you. The grace for the moment is different than a miracle, although it can include a miracle. It is certainly not limited to the miraculous. Sometimes things don't work in the way we want, yet grace for the moment is still present.

At times, our fear and anxiety are unwarranted, because what we are most afraid of will probably never happen — like being afraid to fly. Thousands of flights take off and land each day around the globe. Plane crashes, although devastating to hear about, seldom happen. The United States recently suffered its first fatality on a commercial flight in almost ten years. Those are pretty good statistics, especially compared to the sheer number of automobile accidents, particularly fatal ones.

Let's go back to the example of being afraid to fly. We already talked about how the thing that we fear or dread may never actually happen. What if it does happen? Surely planes have crashed. It is fair to say that those people who experienced a plane crash had their worst fears come true. I say probably not. I say this because, if that thing you are afraid of comes to pass, it usually isn't as bad as you fear.

A friend of mine was on a flight a few years back that experienced engine trouble and had to make an emergency landing. She told us about hearing a loud boom, followed by the pilot's announcement that they would need to turn back to the airport. When I heard her story, I immediately thought about what my reaction would be in that situation. I told her that I probably would have had a heart attack right there in my seat. She agreed with me that that would have been her first reaction upon hearing about a situation like that. However, when she actually experienced it, a surprising calm came over her. She prayed, took deep breaths, and before she knew it, the plane landed. That calm that she felt was her "it". Neither she nor I could have imagined such a thing during an emergency landing. It wasn't for us to imagine. It was for her to experience, only when she needed it — for the moment.

Grace for the moment is the reassurance that nothing comes as a surprise to God. While we are busy worrying, God is busy planning and plotting! He is literally placing yours and my "it" all over!

One thing that I once feared was getting divorced. This one ran deep; deeper than divorce. It came from my lack of self-esteem. I never felt beautiful growing up. I also had a belief instilled in me that a woman was nothing without a man. Marriage represented many things to me. It meant that I was pretty and chosen. It also meant that I had a permanent man. I would never be lonely or have to look for a date! Marriage also represented God and society's approval on my life. I could be many bad things and face many hard trials, but as long as I was married, all would be well!

So, in that context, you see why I couldn't bear the thought of getting married, and then having it ripped from me. In my mind, divorce was an overdose of bad circumstances that took me down from the high of finally belonging and sending me to rock-bottom, back to the pile of life's rejects.

Yet, here I am, divorced. I am still alive, and may I add, thriving!

Listen . . . I am in no way glorifying divorce. But, with or without my glorification of it, it still happens. It happened to me, and I got through it; I was married for a whopping eighteen months! Now, I know that someone may be thinking, "Well, at least you weren't married for twenty years before you got divorced."

Let me tell you that divorce is hard . . . period. While not glorifying it, let's not simplify it either. Do you know how embarrassing it is to get divorced when you are still supposed to be in your honeymoon period? When distant friends or relatives see you and offer congratulations on your recent nuptials, but you didn't even sleep in the same house as your husband the night before? Even now, when I mention to someone about my ex-husband or being divorced, and that person responds with, "I never knew you were married." Trust me . . . whether it was twenty years, or as in my case, just eighteen months, divorce is hard. Yet, it didn't kill me.

While I didn't exactly go skipping to the courthouse to sign my divorce papers, I had a calmness and a peace that truly surpassed my understanding. Everything that I wanted was gone, and that season brought things to me that I didn't want — like seeing another woman pregnant with my husband's child.

The grace for my moment was a buffet of peace, calm, love, blessings, and great achievements that overshadowed the failure of my marriage. God got me through that thing so victoriously that I am ready to do it again (the marriage part, not that divorce thing!)

So, what happens when the plane crashes or the marriage ends? The simple answer is, you either die or you become single! What your dying or singleness looks and feels like can only be experienced in the moment. So please, don't worry about it because God's grace for that moment is already there!

## Prayer For Grace For The Moment

Father God, I thank you for having control over my life. While there are some things that I am uncertain about and even fear, I know that I can give my fears and anxieties over to you. You have never let me down, and you never will. I thank you that wherever I find myself in this life, you have gone before me and will already be there.

Although this includes my mistakes — because where sin exists, grace abounds — I ask for the wisdom to follow your will more closely in my life. I do not always want to be facing consequences; I want to walk in freedom. For me, freedom acknowledges the fact that with you, I have nothing to fear.

I thank you for your grace for the moment. In the name of Jesus, I pray. Amen.

## A Reflection

In this chapter, we discussed grace for the moment. Think of a time when one of your worst fears came true. Was it as awful as you feared? Was there a grace for the moment that helped you to get through it? Did you survive?

_____

_____

_____

_____

_____

_____

_____

_____

# TIMING IS
# EVERYTHING!

> *"Trust in the LORD with all your heart; do not depend on your own understanding. Seek his will in all you do, and he will show you which path to take."*
>
> *—Proverbs 3:5-6 NLT*

**W**hoever *was the first* to say that timing is everything certainly wasn't lying! If you are going to understand how to navigate this life, having a grasp of the importance of time is paramount!

God's will and the timing of God are two distinct entities that must walk lockstep in harmony with each other. If you go against God's will, that's a bad thing. But, going against God's timing is also a bad thing! Take, for example, superstar racecar driver, Jeff Gordon. He rose to international acclaim in a sport that originated as a pastime for country boys who had old car parts lying around! If we agree that NASCAR superstardom was God's will for Jeff Gordon's life, we can also see what role God's timing played in his success.

Let's say that Jeff took it upon himself to get behind the wheel of a race car, or any car for that matter, at the age of five. Unable to touch the pedals and look through the windshield simultaneously, this certainly would have been a recipe for disaster! Jeff could have injured himself to the point of never walking or driving again. He could have been so frightened that he was scarred for life and never got behind the wheel of a car again. The Jeff Gordon that we knew and loved could have been Jeff Gordon, the greeter at Walmart, if he stepped out of God's timing.

While I could write a few chapters to admonish you to go with the flow of God's timing, I would rather share my story. From this story, I want to show you that some things just take time. God hasn't forgotten about you. He has heard your prayers and knows better for you than what you pray about.

In 2014, a woman named Anna, who I have never met, retired from her job as a business manager for a school in Waterbury, CT. Around this same time, I was sitting at my desk at work, contemplating my whole life. At that time, I was working at the same high school that I had graduated from some nineteen years earlier. For years, it felt good to be there. I believed that I had a connection with the students and most of the parents because of my background.

Actually, I knew some of the parents. I was an advocate for the students; most of whom came from the "inner city" (a politically correct way to say poor Black and Latino communities). The students' neighborhoods couldn't be further in distance and demographics than most of the teachers. As someone from the inner city, and as I mentioned, a graduate of the school, I connected with the kids and earned a great deal of respect.

Connection aside, soon, the nostalgia and the novelty began to wear off by 2014. I felt stuck. The straight-A student, who was the valedictorian of her class, now sat in a cubicle in the same high school's main office. Is this what becomes of a valedictorian — the math whiz who went to college on a full four-year academic scholarship? The girl who was encouraged by her teacher to apply to Harvard (I didn't)? The future engineer who was shocked when MIT wanted to interview her (I didn't go)? I started to feel like the basketball star who still tells the same story twenty years later of how he scored the game-winning basket; the dude with limp muscles and a beer gut. Who puts on a pair of too-small basketball shorts and challenges the younger guys to a game of "Let's see if I still got it!"?

Twenty years after high school, nobody cares that you got straight A's. Twenty years after high school, no one cares about the colleges you were accepted into. No one was impressed by the full four-year scholarship that I didn't fully utilize because I dropped out after the first year. They didn't care. I thought they cared that the girl who was unanimously voted as the most likely to succeed was the first face they saw when they returned to their old high school to get a copy of their transcript.

Okay, let's be honest, they probably didn't care about that either — that was all me. I cared. I hated it and doggone it, I was going to do something about it...

*Or, so I thought.*

One day, while I was getting ready to fax perhaps my third in a series of application packets, the Lord spoke to me. He said, "You don't leave when it gets hard. You leave if, and when, I tell you to."

I heard Him loud and clear. And while I'd be lying if I said that I always obeyed the voice of the Lord, this time I did. I knew that my job search would be an exercise in futility if I continued. I would have wasted time and paper mailing or faxing job applications and resumes. I wasn't going to get an interview. Or worse, and this really scared me, I could disobey God and keep applying for jobs. Only to end up someplace where I did not belong. And not just a place where I didn't fit in, but in a place of disobedience.

Did a nice salary and corner office mean that much to me that I would blatantly disobey God? The answer was no. So, I stayed and waited for further instructions. Was it easy? It most certainly was not. But I stayed. I had no idea what I was waiting for. One thing that I was sure of was that I knew how to do my boss' job. I was ready to be in that position. But she was nowhere near retiring. So, I stayed. This was 2014. While I was sitting there, obeying God, yet feeling sorry for myself, a woman named Anna was submitting her retirement papers.

Now, if you think you know where this story is going, let me stop you right there. No, I did not take Anna's job. A woman named Susan took Anna's job. Susan was the business manager of a high school in Meriden, CT, and started her new job sometime in 2015; her previous position sat vacant for the better part of a year — nearly ten months. So, was it Susan's job that was waiting for me? Nope! I didn't take Susan's job either. A woman named Martha took Susan's old job. Martha was the business manager of a high school in Milford. She worked there for twenty-six years and loved it.

That was until 2014, when a new principal took over. Well, he wasn't exactly a new principal; he had worked at several high schools in the district during the past few decades. His most recent appointment was as the principal of the high school where I worked. I remember when he left in 2014. He had only been there for two years, so I didn't get a chance to know him — that and the fact that I felt invisible to him. I used to joke and say that when he looked at my desk, all he saw was a chair. . . and not me sitting in it!

My boss at the time didn't help that. If I completed a report, drafted a letter, or anything, I had to give it to her first, then she would present it to the principal. No wonder the man thought I was invisible.

*Or, so I thought.*

In 2016, when Martha left her position as a business manager in a high school in Milford, CT, the principal immediately sought to replace her. He didn't have to ask around because he knew who he wanted — he wanted me! Not my chair, but me! Not my boss, but me! So, in 2016, I left my job at my former high school and walked into a promotional position as the business manager!

I didn't know it back then, but when God told me not to leave, He knew! He knew who would retire . . . and who would transfer, and eventually leave an open spot for me!

## Timing!

I have no clue how long Anna had planned to retire. She probably pondered over it for years, like many employees. Eventually, she did retire. And a chain of events took place that ultimately brought me to a job that I didn't even have to apply for! That's the power of the will of God perfectly syncing with the timing of God!

I want to encourage you today in your waiting. We are taught to hustle, grind, and get busy for what we want. And there is a time and season to do that. Let's ponder this thought for a moment. When you hustle too hard and chase too hard, it is possible to run past the promise God has for you! While you are chasing, running at full speed, the promise is sitting still. It is in a place in time. Time is a stop along the railway of your life. One day, you will be riding along, wondering when you will reach your destination, when all of a sudden, the conductor pulls into a station and says, "It's time!" Time will board the train, shake hands with God's will, and live happily ever after!

That's how the story goes. The key is to not get off of the train in frustration. Stay on the train. If you run out of money, stay on the train. If friends and family members stop riding with you, let them go; you just be sure to stay on the train.

# Prayer For Timing Is Everything

Father God, I thank you for your will being done in my life. I ask for the patience to let things play out and not rush it. I do not know what is going on behind the scenes, but I trust that no good thing will you withhold from me. I pray for the peace to not go ahead of you, but to consistently trust you in all things. In the name of Jesus, I pray. Amen.

## A Reflection

In this chapter, we discussed that timing is everything. Have you ever gotten something before you were ready for it? Have you waited for something, and when it finally showed up, you realized why you had to wait? What are you waiting for now? Instead of rushing to get it, take time to pray about it. Let God instruct you on how to wait or how to go get it. Write down what you hear in prayer.

_____

_____

_____

_____

_____

_____

_____

_____

# YOUR FIRST IMPRESSION MAY BE WRONG!

> *"Spouting off before listening to the facts is both shameful and foolish."*
>
> —*Proverbs 18:13 NLT*

ost of us have heard the expression, "you never get a second chance to make a first impression". Many people swear by this and make it their life's motto. But is it a good motto to live by? Is it even an accurate statement? In my experience (and again, I am writing about what I know, not about what I don't know), this statement doesn't hold true enough for me to live by it. A statement such as this doesn't allow for any kind of grace.

We cannot make up for a bad first impression; nor can someone else be forgiven for rubbing us the wrong way. This is in no way excusing a bad impression left upon you by someone's bad behavior. Instead, I want us to look at the fact that we could be, and just might be, wrong about what we see in a person.

In this life, you will need people. Solitude and isolation certainly have their place in our lives. However, you cannot be in permanent solitude or isolation. Just as occasional fasting is good, but permanent fasting leads to death.

## Love God... love people

Not only do we need people, but we've been called to love people. Whether you are the world's biggest extrovert or the quiet, reserved type, we need to know how to get along with people. One way to get along with people is to meet them halfway. Give them a break. Go the extra mile. The best way to do this is to understand that some of the best people to come into your life may not be the smiling, happy, helpful type. If you run away from difficult people, or people who don't necessarily lay out the red carpet for you each time you walk by, you could be missing out on connections, lessons, or solutions.

Johanna, who was once my supervisor at a job that I held for four years, has evolved into my mentor and role model. This beautiful woman of God is a great wife, wonderful mother, and one of the "baddest" bosses to ever work this side of the moon. She has probably lost count of how many times she has been promoted, having started her career as an entry-level clerk and retiring as a second-level Fiscal Manager. She went from earning minimum wage to nearly $70/hour, managing a staff of thirty professionals, and handling a budget of approximately $50 million. She's bad, y'all. And when I first met her, I thought she was really bad.

In 2004, I was at an office for an interview. There is a whole testimony about that statement alone that may — or may not — make it into this book. Anyway, I was in an interview with one department, and things were going great. They talked with me as if I had the job already. But, even with them being impressed with my skill set, they felt that I would be a better fit in the business office. The man who was a part of my interview team excused himself and ran to the business office to urge them to interview me right away and not to let me leave!

Well, as you can imagine, with such a boost of confidence from this man, I walked into this next interview, ready to take them by storm! This interview panel also consisted of a man and a woman. The man was very impressed by me; he smiled and nodded the entire time, and I knew that I had won him over. The woman in the interview, Johanna, did not crack a smile, and she asked me to explain or expound on every answer that I gave. They took turns asking me questions, but when it was the man's turn to ask me something, Johanna threw in her two cents.

Needless to say, my mood changed from expecting and hopeful to doubtful and uncomfortable. Fortunately for me, I didn't have a thing to worry about! Johanna loved me and offered me the job later on that afternoon. When she called my boss for a reference, she couldn't say enough great things about me.

The four years that I worked under Johanna were some of the best years of my career. She taught me everything she knew because she was, in fact, grooming me for her job. We grew close on a personal level too. She taught me many things about faith and family, never going on any trip without bringing back a gift for me. I had her screen a boyfriend for my ex-husband and me. She gave me the thumbs down on both of them — and she was right!

On the day of my interview, I had no idea what God had in store for me through Johanna. And, thank God I didn't walk out of the interview or have a nasty attitude when answering her questions. I came to know her to be a woman of high standards. Or perhaps, she was just handling business, and it was something in me that needed a smiling, nurturing voice to soothe me. That was my problem, not hers. I was wrong about her.

Another example of being wrong about a first impression happened one year when I bought a car. I was looking through a magazine that listed cars for sale. I had narrowed it down to two cars that I liked, so I called each dealership to inquire about the vehicle. When I called the first dealership, the man who answered the phone was short with me and kind of impatient. He invited me to come to the lot and check out the car for myself, but he certainly wasn't interested in spending ten minutes on the phone with me to give me every detail about the vehicle. I thought he was rude, so I called another used car lot. The man who answered the phone at the second dealership was the polar opposite of the first guy. This man told me everything I wanted to know about the car. He was patient, kind, and even said "God bless you" at the end of the phone call! Well, that was an easy decision for me. I would buy my car from the nice guy.

As it turns out, the car that I bought from the nice guy was a total lemon! Yes, it was a used car, but he had deceived me! He was supposed to fix a problem with the car that was indicated by one of the dashboard lights. However, instead of fixing the problem, he managed to remove a fuse and turn the indicator light off! Unbelievable, right? Remember, this guy was patient, kind and said God bless you!

Eventually, I found myself shopping for a car again, and I somehow ended up going to dealership number one — the one with the guy who I thought was rude because he didn't have time to talk on the phone with me. Boy, was I wrong about him! He wasn't rude at all. He was busy! He owned a garage and used car dealership that was thriving because he had customers. . . real, satisfied customers who came back to him and referred their friends. I forgot to mention that at the other dealership; I was always the only customer there the times that I went to test drive the car and buy it. No wonder he had time to sit and chat on the phone with me (and say God bless you!). The car that I bought from the second dealership was impeccable! I drove it for three years before I traded it in for a new car. They sold it to me for a fair price and let me split the down payment into three payments, but I was able to drive away once I paid the first installment. I don't know if they are still in business, but if they are, I would definitely recommend them to anyone looking for a used car.

I cried when I thought of the trouble, time, and money I could have saved if I had just gone to this dealership in the first place. I let my first impression of them get in the way. Again, I attributed this to something in me that didn't like professional, straight-to-the-point or busy people!

When life hands you something that you don't want, it doesn't hurt to look at yourself first. You are not always the victim, and other people are not always to blame. I believe that we project and reflect our own emotions and mindset onto other people. Because something in me was broken, I always needed someone to fix me or speak softly to me. That brokenness led me down the wrong path more than once. I chose people who spoke a certain way to me and dismissed others. I couldn't see the bigger picture. I trusted the guy who said 'God bless you' instead of asking my own mechanic to look at the car first.

Knowing that you might be wrong about someone frees you to give them another chance. You can still form a friendship with them. You can go back and buy a fabulous car from them. We are not in bondage to first impressions; I don't care how long we've been using that statement!

## Prayer For Your First Impression May Be Wrong

Father God, I thank you for giving me the wisdom to deal with people in all situations. Help me to love someone who may have rubbed me the wrong way. Please deal with the inner parts of me that only want to deal with people who are extra nice, motherly, fatherly, etc. Help me to understand that everyone has a story, and that everyone has a reason for the way they are.

Please heal me from racism, sexism, classism, any other prejudice that I have against people. These prejudices paint the first impression of someone before they get a chance to prove themselves. I realize that some of my greatest blessings will often come through unexpected avenues, including people who I never expected to be a blessing. Lord, I am open to be more loving and accepting.

I thank you that people will also be more open to me and extend grace to me, if I should not make a great impression on them the first time we meet. In the name of Jesus, I pray. Amen.

## A Reflection

In this chapter, we discussed that our first impression of someone could be wrong. Can you recall a time when you judged a person or a situation wrong? Have you been judged and dismissed by someone who had you all wrong? Is there a person or a situation that you don't like now, that perhaps you can offer grace and see the good in them?

_____

_____

_____

_____

_____

_____

_____

_____

# HOLD OFF ON YOUR JUDGMENTS

*"There is a path before each person that seems right, but it ends in death."*

—Proverbs 14:12 NLT

*"And we know that God causes everything to work together for the good of those who love God and are called according to his purpose for them."*

—Romans 8:28 NLT

L ife is going to throw things at you. That is the premise of this whole book. But, another way to not let the things that life throws at you to get you down is to hold off on your good or bad judgments. That may sound like a mantra for the New Age school of peace, love, and freedom! And it, in fact, might be their mantra! But, it's a pretty good way to navigate through life. When something happens to you or you experience a life event, you cannot judge the thing as being either good or bad at the onset.

## You just can't! Here's why!

Life has shown us that too many good things have come from bad things. And vice versa, many bad things work out for an unanticipated good. Bad that works out for the good. Let's start with the latter point for discussion: Have you ever had anything that seemed bad at first, then turned out to be a good thing?

- A person rejects you or breaks your heart. In doing so, they freed you to meet the love of your life.
- You are not chosen for a job that seemed so perfect. Then the company downsizes and would have left you unemployed.
- You get a bad diagnosis from your doctor. Yet, it is the very thing that helps you to finally lose weight, stop smoking, etc. and get your health in order.
- You get fired, and it pushes you to finally start your own business.
- You are put in an impossible situation. Then you experience a true miracle that would not have manifested otherwise.

There was a book that was popular more than twenty years ago. It was titled, "We got fired! And it's the Best Thing that Ever Happened to Us!" The book gives biographical accounts of job loss by some pretty big names. Each person gives tricks and tips on how to turn to bounce back and turn your defeat into dreams.

I have never read the book. Just the title alone is intriguing enough that I heard about it decades ago, and still remember it today! And, although the book was geared towards teaching movers and shakers how to keep moving and shaking, it is practical advice for anyone. Yet, beyond that timeless, practical advice, is the idea that bad often turns out to be good without moving or shaking a thing!

If God really wanted you to leave your job, would you? Your answer may be an unequivocal "Yes," and that's great. It's also okay if you aren't sure what you would do because, if God wants to close a door in your life and move you towards a better direction, He doesn't need your permission. Many things that we label as bad bring us to the good, even great, places that we would not have gone to otherwise.

Mothers Against Drunk Driving (MADD) was founded in 1980 by a woman named Candace Lightner. She started the organization after her thirteen-year-old daughter was killed by a drunk driver. Today, there is at least one MADD office in every state in the country and Canada. MADD has over four hundred employees and more than eight thousand volunteers. The organization is responsible for literally reducing the amount of drunk driving-related deaths by half! If you consider that there were twenty-seven thousand drunk driving-related deaths at the time the organization was founded, MADD has helped to save the lives of about three hundred seventy-eight thousand people!

Losing her daughter was certainly no good thing, but her death was not in vain. It's doubtful that Mrs. Lightner would have begun the organization otherwise. I thank her for this!

We have no way of knowing if drunk driving laws and practices are why we are still alive today!

I had an experience of being fired from a job. For full disclosure, I wasn't fired due to layoffs or mistreatment. I did something wrong, and I paid the price. In fact, the thing that I did was not only wrong, but no one had ever done it before, so there was no precedent on the actions to take. My employer let me work for three days while they figured out if I needed to be fired and under which pretense. I said all of that to say that I wasn't an innocent party at all. Some innocent employees could have been fired along with me.

Thankfully, they were not. Anyway, at the time of my being fired, I worked two jobs. My other job was as a part-time clerk typist with the State of Connecticut. Working for the government has long been considered a good job — great pay, great benefits, etc. But, unfortunately, my job with the State was only fifteen hours a week. Not enough for a single mother and her son to live off of. Yet, I was told by more than one person that God wanted me to give up one of my jobs and trust him. Obviously, my full-time job would be the one to let go of. Otherwise, it would not have been a walk of faith.

Nevertheless, I held on to both jobs until the night in July 2004 when I was fired. It was nighttime because I worked third shift at the time, so when I reported to work at nine o'clock p.m.., I was met by a supervisor who brought me into the office and told me to clean out my desk. I knew something was up when I saw his car in the lot because he never worked at night. Three days before this, I prayed. I prayed the prayer that anyone would pray when they've been caught doing something wrong and risked losing their job. I, of course, prayed to keep my job.

Well, one minute into a sobbing, tearful, heartfelt prayer, God interrupted me. His response to my plea was, "But, Ann-Gela, you don't even like this job!" True, I didn't like it. I didn't like working overnight. I hated the superior attitudes of the supervisors. You name it, and I could tell you how much I didn't like it. But I was faced with the decision to leave the full-time for my part-time, or my eventually being fired. The job looked pretty nice. Safe, comfortable, and reliable (that was until I got fired).

In November 2004, about four months after I was fired, I was hired full-time by a state agency (please see my story about my boss, Johanna!) The new full-time job doubled the salary of the job I was fired from. Two years later, I was promoted and add another $15,000 to my salary.

Six years after that, I was promoted once more, which increased my salary by $20,000, which is significant because that was the yearly salary of my old job — the one that I had been fired from. The one I was afraid to let go of. The one that I prayed to keep. The one where, if and when I was ever promoted, would never earn the salary that I earn today. There just wasn't room for that type of growth in that company. I had no idea on that rainy night back in July 2004 that I would be able to honestly write today, *thank God that I was fired!*

I must also tell you that when I was fired, I didn't go home right away. No one was expecting me until morning anyway. So, I drove to the parking lot of the grocery store and cried. I contemplated taking my severance check and hitting the highway and not look back. Then, I thought that my son would be devastated if I disappeared. But, how could I take him with me with a four-hundred-dollar check and probably the same amount in the bank? Then I figured I'd kill myself. Or at least try. So, I bought a bottle of Tylenol PM. There were twenty-four pills in the bottle. Don't laugh at my suicide attempt. I have no idea if those twenty-four pills would have been enough to do the job. I bought the bottle and decided to drive to the emergency room. My plan was to swallow the pills in the parking lot, then immediately go inside to tell them what I had done. If they could save me, great. If not, oh well.

I never took the pills. In fact, I eventually returned them to the store for a refund! That bottle cost $4.99, and I was now unemployed, so I needed that money! Instead, that night I drove to a friend's house and cried on her shoulders (Thanks, Keisha!). I went to the gym as soon as they opened at five a.m. and worked out for about an hour. Then, I went home and told my mother what happened. I knew the next day would be hard. But I walked through it. Then, I got up the day after that and walked through that one, too. And I kept walking as days turned to weeks, and months, and finally fourteen years later, as I sit here and type this story.

I've done many things since then that I am not proud of. But, one thing I haven't done is gotten fired ever again!

*It was good that I was afflicted.*

When bad things happen, pause, pray, and reflect. It may not be such a bad thing, after all. Hold off on your judgment until this thing has really played out. At the very least, it will ease your stress and help with the pain of what you are facing. It's working out for your good. Just you wait and see.

I think that the immediate judgment of something to be good has caused more trouble than we can imagine. How can any of the following things ever become bad?

- A new job with a six-figure salary.
- The opportunity to go to college.
- A handsome or beautiful person who shows a strong interest in you.
- Winning money.
- Finding the perfect house.
- Being offered a new ministry assignment.
- A work-from-home job.
- A super easy diet and exercise plan.
- A new car.

At first glance, each of these things seems like a great thing to have! Let's look closely at a few of these great things!

## A new job with a six-figure salary

No one would argue that a new job with a six-figure salary is a bad thing, right? But, did they tell you that you would have to work nights and weekends, and often travel on your own dime? Who cares, because you are making all of that money? That's until you discover that your spouse resents you, your kids miss you, and your boss doesn't respect you the way they should.

## The opportunity to go to college

I went to college, as did my oldest son. College opened many doors of opportunity, both professionally and personally. Now, my son graduated with very little debt; his student loan balance was less than what I expected to repay each year. I say expected because, like countless other students, I often fell behind in payments.

If this was a book solely about financial planning, I would really drop some nuggets here, but to keep it short, consider the cost before you do it. Don't get caught up in the status of the school. Don't take more than five years to graduate. If you are having a hard time deciding a major, it's best to take a break then pay for years while you explore different classes. Also, don't be surprised if, after all of the money and time that you spent getting your degree, you find yourself working for someone with no degree at all!

## Winning money

*"I won the lottery, and it ruined my life!"* No, not me. I didn't win; that's the name of a reality show. The show is all about people who won huge jackpots and eventually had their lives go down the tubes. While winning millions of dollars, or even just one million dollars, seems like the answer to your prayers, money brings problems that you cannot imagine

while you are broke. Not only does money bring its own set of problems, the problems that you had before the money will still be there.

## Prayer For Hold Off On Your Good Or Bad Judgments

Father God, my life is in your hand. I surrender to your will for my life. God, I pray that I allow you to be in control. Your ways are higher than my ways, and your thoughts are higher than my thoughts. When something comes into my life or something happens in my life, I pray for the wisdom to seek your judgment of a thing. I pray to follow the voice and direction of the Holy Spirit.

Lord, I know that many bad things come dressed up in good packages. And I know that blessings are often hidden in the circumstances or places that I don't want to go. Yet, God, my prayer is that I trust you. Give me the courage to walk away from a good thing that you warn me about. And give me the faith to stick around and tough it out in a bad situation that you assure me will be alright.

It's no longer about what I think or feel; it is all about surrender to your will. I thank you, Father, for this new insight. In the name of Jesus, I pray.

Amen.

## A Reflection

In this chapter, we discussed not judging people, places, or circumstances at the onset. Have you experienced seeing something as a bad thing that actually turned out to be good? How about something that looked good, but the end result of it was bad? What have these experiences taught you?

_____

_____

_____

_____

_____

_____

_____

_____

_____

_____

_____

_____

_____

# How I Learned To Overcome Jealousy And Envy

> "Let your conversation be without covetousness; and be content with such things as ye have: for he hath said, I will never leave thee, nor forsake thee."
>
> —Hebrews 13:5 KJV

O*ne of the surest* ways to be unhappy with your life is to be jealous and envious of someone. Webster's dictionary defines jealousy as "being worried that someone will take what you have (your spouse, your attention from the boss)". Envy is "wanting what someone else has".

Although they are defined differently, jealousy and envy often walk hand-in-hand. Regardless of which one you may be feeling, these emotions keep you in a state of being ungrateful. You never feel like your life is enough. You blame God for skipping over you. You become angry at the person for having what you desire. Or the person may have the same as you but are jealous because you had to earn it, and they just walked into it. Here are three ways that I was able to overcome jealousy and envy and have a more peaceful life.

*People will tell you what they did, but they won't always tell you how they did it.*

This was a very big lesson for me to learn. I would get envious of someone who was married, had a nice house, a great job, an awesome ministry, or even a great body. But the thing was just a thing — it was a result, a consequence. There is always a story to the story. Sometimes that story involves prayer, fasting, hard work, sacrifice, etc., etc., blah, blah, blah! I say that because, for every story of hard work and dedication, there are also a thousand backstories:

> The person with the great shape isn't in the gym every day. They were born with a great metabolism, or they recently had weight loss surgery!

> The couple with the beautiful, big home didn't scrimp and save for years. They won the lotto or received an inheritance.

> The person who seems happily married really isn't. Or, they are happy, but little did you know that this is marriage number three for them because the third time's the charm!

A few years ago, while I was unemployed, I went to my credit union to close my account and to withdraw what little money I had in there. At the teller next to me, a man also withdrew money, but he inquired about his balance first. Well, while I was taking the last $150 I had to my name, this guy's balance was more than $11,000. I remember being jealous, envious, angrious (not a word, but it just flows). But, that $11,000 could have come from an income tax refund. Or, perhaps that $11,000 was previously $50,000, but the IRS put a lien on his account. There I was, jealous of this man, but what if he owed a bookie $15,000? I was jealous of him, and at the same time, he's afraid for his life.

I remembered when I first realized that people don't tell you everything. They only tell you what they want you to know. A former friend of mine used to always brag about money. She couldn't wait to tell you how blessed she was, how she always had money in the bank, and could easily show you the stack of $20 and $50 bills in her wallet. Yes, she worked hard, but she didn't make that much money. She wasn't a doctor or a Wall Street broker, or anything like that. She wore designer clothes and went out to eat a lot, so I never saw where she budgeted or saved her money.

Then one day, I found out part of her secret. I knew that the father of her eldest child had passed away when her daughter was just a baby. Well, my friend conveniently forgot to mention the nice sum of money that she received each month from Social Security. The extra $1,000 a month explained a lot. That, and the fact that she would regularly buy food stamps from a family member for fifty cents on the dollar! No wonder she had such an extra cash flow each month. Now, imagine if I had been jealous of her or tried to keep up with her lifestyle! I would have made a fool of myself attempting to mimic what she did without her resources.

Before you get jealous of someone and try to keep up with the Jones', remember that the Jones' haven't told you everything, and they probably never will.

## Nobody has it all together.

This concept will help you with the first one. People will surely leave out important details in their lives. The reasons for their privacy is only known to them. But, it's very likely that people neglect to tell you their mistakes or things they are embarrassed to share. Honestly, whether you are aware of a person's shortcomings or not, rest assured, they are there.

Now, this isn't a case of misery loving company, and I'm not encouraging you to stay in your bad situation because "everyone has bad things in their life." No, if anything, I am encouraging you to keep pressing forward, in spite of the pitfalls and obstacles in your life. Often times, jealousy comes on the scene when we feel that everyone else has it easier. That is simply not true. So, don't be jealous — get out there and be great!

At the time of my writing this book, I am currently a single parent of a very active and inquisitive five-year-old. His dad and I split for the fiftieth time back in 2016. At that time, he told me that if we weren't together, that he wouldn't really be involved with his son. He wasn't lying. He has made very good on his promise. So, by the grace of God, I am parenting without a partner. I work full-time in a very demanding job. I am a manager, and while that sounds glorious, it really means that everybody's job is really my job.

I have to train, orientate, correct, and cover for every position that I oversee. I have a great staff, but rest assured, they take days off that I can't. They make mistakes that I have to answer for. And they are quick to remind me of what is and what isn't their job.

I leave the house at seven o'clock each morning to get my son to his before-school program by seven fifteen, and then head to work in order to arrive by seven forty-five. I get off of work at four fifteen, but my son gets out of school at three o'clock. His school doesn't have a bus, so thankfully, I am able to pay for a cab that transports him to his after-school program. My son stays at the program until after five o'clock each day. He has a longer day than some adults. My son also participates in karate, science programs, and now, baseball for the season. I am grateful. I am blessed, but I am also tired. My son's room is the laundry room. It is the place where clean and dry clothes go to wait to be folded. Okay . . . let me not lie . . . the clothes never get folded! I go in there each night and rummage for clothes for us to wear the next day.

In addition to laundry, there may or may not be dishes in my sink at this moment. I vacuum at random intervals. I used Magic Scrubbing Bubbles to keep my shower from becoming a germ bath. And I forgot to take our trash cans to the curb last night, so I'll be stuffing the bags down in order to make room for more until next week. I basically neglect my home-based business until a customer needs to reorder. I manage to exercise five times a week because I do it on my lunch break at work. I also leave work early once a month to get my hair done or to get a pedicure. I am thankful for the babysitters that I can call on when needed. Still, there have been times when I wanted to call them, but really couldn't afford it.

Yet, when I go to work, church, or just about anywhere, people stop and compliment me on my look and my pleasant demeanor. Honestly, I have a knack for putting together outfits that compliment me. I can also do my makeup in five minutes; I have even brought it to work with me to put on in the bathroom on several occasions. I am happy because I am blessed. I am happy because I am gifted, talented, and hopeful. I know that one day I'll be married again. I pray for a great relationship with my in-laws. I pray for a host of aunties and uncles and friends who will assist with parenting. While I make good money, I pray for a few streams of residual income that will allow for a housekeeper, nanny, and ensure every bill is paid on time. BUT, until these additional things come to pass, I am grateful for what I get to do. So, I get up, I dress up, I look up, and I write books!

Nobody has it all together. No need to wait for "their life." Go on out there with what you have and be great!

## What God has for you . . . is for you!

Let's revisit the definition of the words jealousy and envy. Jealousy is being worried that someone will take what you have. Envy is wanting what someone else has. When we feel jealous or envious, what we are really feeling is overlooked or forgotten by God. No one can rightfully take that which is yours. And you do not have to want what someone else has because there is plenty more to go around. If, by chance, the last thing is given to someone else, trust and believe that God can create more!

While it can be painful to watch other people enjoy and experience things that you may long for, it will help you to know, one day, you may get to enjoy those same things.

Or not. Maybe you won't get to enjoy those exact same things or experiences. That doesn't mean that God has overlooked or forgotten you. You will get to enjoy the things that God has for you. No good thing will he withheld from you.

Years ago, I read an article in a magazine entitled "Thirty things that every adult must do before they turn 30". While I certainly cannot remember the entire list, I do remember a few items; such as work at a real "nine-to-five" job for at least five years, have a passport, and travel out of the country at least once. If you have this list, or one similar to it, throw it away!

Some people become parents for the first time at sixteen. Others become parents for the first time in their forties. Both will have to pay for diapers! Some folks married their high school sweethearts. I know of couples who found each other later in life -- much later in life! You might rise through the ranks and become the top boss in your career at a young age. Or you may retire as the boss' assistant. Both are jobs that pay real money!

Prayer is the key that unlocks the peace of knowing who you are and what your purpose is. Life is a journey. Enjoy the journey. Stop looking at life as a checklist full of impending deadlines — if God promised you two things in this world, rest assured that those two promises are coming to pass. Walking in the fullness of those promises feels better than trying to achieve everything on a list.

## Prayer For How I Learned To Overcome Jealousy

Father God, everyone else seems to have more, be doing more, living better, and not facing any hardship. I know in my heart that this isn't true. No one has a perfect life, and we all have issues to face. God, please help me not to want what someone else has. Truth be told, I don't know how they got it, and I may be unable or unwilling to do what they did. So, obviously, it isn't for me. All of the time that I spend admiring someone else's life takes away from fully enjoying my own life.

Forgive me, Lord. I declare today that I am enough, that I have enough, and most importantly, you are enough for me. I am grateful and thankful for all that you have given me. Help me to appreciate the people, places, and things that you have blessed me with. I am blessed, loved, and taken care of. Thank you, Father. In the name of Jesus, I pray. Amen.

## A Reflection

In this chapter, we discussed Jealousy and Envy. Be honest with yourself. Have you ever been jealous or envious of someone? Were you jealous of someone who seemed to have had it all together, and you later learned that that was not the case? Are you jealous of someone now? What steps can you take to ease your jealousy and walk in freedom?

# FIND THE LESSON IN EVERYTHING

> *"For everyone who asks, receives. Everyone who seeks, finds. And to everyone who knocks, the door will be opened."*
>
> —Matthew 7:8 NLT

L*ast year, I tried* online dating for the first time. Actually, it was my second time. But the first go-round was a waste of time and money, so in my book, it doesn't count. Anyway, moving on... this time around, I woke up the morning after I set-up my profile to eighteen messages, and each day after that, I received messages and notifications of guys giving me the thumbs up!

Eventually the messages warranted taking it offline, and I took a chance to get to know four guys. Now, for the sake of full disclosure, when I say that I got to *know* them, I am not referring to the biblical sense!

Again, moving right along . . . Out of the four guys that I met, there was one that I really liked. Although I liked him as a person, I didn't like the way things were going in our relationship. In fact, I should not have referred to it as a relationship. It was a thing, a fling, a "situationship" (you can judge me if you want to, but I'm the one telling the story here, so you just have to read it). We were heading towards the three-month mark, and it was time to have a conversation — not just any conversation, but *thee* conversation. We needed to discuss where we were going. Are we going to be a couple? Am I just wasting my time?

His answer: He liked where we were. He wanted to continue to date and keep it light. Oh, and he also still had feelings for his ex-girlfriend. He also had lunch with this ex-girlfriend . . . and happy hour and spent a few Saturday mornings cheering on her son's soccer team! In other words, they had what I would call a full-fledged relationship! No wonder he didn't really have one with me.

This hurt me more than I thought it would. I purposely kept it light with him; a casual dating situation that we could choose to end or go further with at any time. I almost went into complete victim mode. I could have bashed him, called him a dog, and accused him of stringing me along while still dealing with his ex. But, one day, as I was standing at the kitchen sink washing dishes, I realized that I had grown. Had this been a few years prior, I would have kept seeing him. I would have asked him, or even checked his phone to see if he had spoken to his ex that day. I would have tried to lose weight, buy him gifts, cook him a five-star meal, or even exhaust myself trying to blow his mind in the bedroom — all for attention in the name of competition.

Now mind you, as I stated earlier, the relationship wasn't going the way I wanted it to. Honestly, when I first joined the online dating site, I really wanted to get dressed up and go out on fabulous dates. I had hoped to meet men who loved opera, museums, and fine dining. I planned to spend Friday nights with 'Tyler' at a quaint jazz spot.

Then Saturday night would be with 'Oscar' at a Broadway show. By Sunday afternoon, I would be found hiking with 'Shawn' and hitting up a juice bar.

When my dates with this guy began to follow the consistent pattern of his house, my house, and a trip to the diner in between our houses, I realized that this wasn't what I wanted or imagined.

### And I was able to walk away.

I had never done that before. I had held onto relationships, flings, and "situationships" until they imploded and sent pieces of my heart flying in all directions. Not this time. This time, I was thankful that I knew what I wanted and was able to tell myself *this ain't it*.

When life comes at you in unpleasant ways, being the victim or the host of the pity party may have been your go-to response. But, to really navigate the roads of life, you have to look at everything for what it's worth. Sometimes it's a blessing, other times it's a lesson. Take it for what it is and move into the next season.

That failed business? No sweat. I guarantee that you are more equipped to teach a class on Business 101 than any young Ivy League business school graduate. Take those lessons and improve your next venture. Relationship troubles? Legal troubles? Financial troubles? What can you learn from this experience that will keep you from having to experience it again and allow you to move forward?

Get to know a person before you trust them. Pay your bills on time. Don't get texts while driving. Whatever the lesson(s) may be, for certain, there is a lesson to learn from everything and everyone who comes into your life.

## Prayer For Find the Lesson In Everything

Father God, I know by now that not everything in life is going to go my way. Yet, I know that there is a lesson to be learned in everything. Help me to learn from all of my difficult situations. Help me to also know how to let go because nothing in life is permanent. Everything comes into my life for a reason or a season. Let me never be too prideful to ask, "What can I learn from this?" Let me never be too prideful to let go of people or things that have served their purpose in my life.

Lord, I turn this difficult situation over to you. It is difficult for me, but nothing is too hard for you. I pray for the guidance of the Holy Spirit to teach me how to learn, let go, walk away, and do better next time. In the name of Jesus, I pray. Amen.

### A Reflection

In this chapter, we discussed finding the lesson in everything. There is a school of thought that believes that nothing is happening to us, but everything is happening for us. It's new age in origin; however, the Bible states this same thought in Romans 8:28. What are some lessons that you learned from hard times or unpleasant experiences? Are you currently experiencing something difficult? Perhaps looking for the lesson can help you go through it.

_____

_____

_____

_____

_____

_____

_____

_____

_____

_____

_____

_____

_____

_____

_____

_____

_____

# COUNT
# YOUR BLESSINGS

> *"And give thanks for everything to God the Father in the name of our Lord Jesus Christ."*
>
> *—Ephesians 5:20 NLT*

O*ne way to talk* your way out of a bad situation and change your mindset is to count your blessings. Life and death lie in the power of the tongue, so, always remember that your words matter. For some reason, Proverbs 15:1 comes to mind: "A soft answer turns away wrath, but grievous words stir up anger." I've always referred to this Scripture in terms of interpersonal relationships.

However, what if we used this Scripture as a reminder to be careful of what we say in a bad situation. When something goes wrong in our life, it can be tempting to focus on it and constantly talk about it. The words that we use in a difficult situation can either make the situation better or worse.

One morning when my son was still very much a baby, we were heading out the door when I realized that he had made a mess in his diaper. I didn't really have time to change him if I wanted to make it to work on time. And, I also knew better than to send him to daycare like that. So, I laid him on the bed to change him. Of course, you know that this wasn't a simple, easy task. His poop had leaked through his diaper and was all over his back. Clean up required me to get him completely undressed, clean him, wash him up, and redress him. All while racing against the clock and praying that no baby poop made its way onto my good work clothes!

At that moment, I remember feeling overwhelmed, lonely, and a whole bunch of other emotions. Between tears and clean up, I asked myself the following questions: Why did he have to poop now? Why wasn't his dad around to help me? Why do I have to take my baby to strangers at a daycare? Why don't I have a nanny? Why do I even have to work and leave my baby all day? These questions had all the makings of the invitation to a very familiar pity party. So, before I went off the deep end, I began to count my blessings. Thank God that my baby could poop. That means that his digestive system is working. He was a breastfed baby, so it was hard to tell how much milk he drank. Regular pooping is a sign that he's eating and eliminating. Thank God!

Then I thanked God that my arms and legs worked. I wasn't helpless. I could help myself, and more importantly, I could help my baby. I had a job — a well-paying job. I had a nice, late model car. I could see, and therefore, could drive myself and my baby wherever we needed to go! Talk about being blessed! By the time I finished counting my blessings and praising God...

Pity turned into power! Tears were replaced with triumph! I went from feeling overwhelmed to being overjoyed!

*And I made it to work on time!*

At times, when it feels like your whole world is coming down around you, rest assured that it is not. Start counting your blessings as a way to clear your head; make gratitude a regular part of your day. One tip that I find helpful when I'm having a bad time is to say the opposite of what I might be feeling or want to say:

> Instead of saying, "I'm overwhelmed," say, "I have all that I need."
>
> Instead of saying, "I'm broke," say, "I thank God for supplying all of my needs."
>
> Instead of saying, "I'm lonely," say, "I'm thankful for my family and friends, especially those that I haven't met yet!"

This helps you to take nothing for granted. Because, believe me, no matter how small or insignificant something in your life seems, you would be devastated if you didn't have it. Don't take people, places, or things for granted. You will miss them when they're gone.

One more nugget . . . don't lose what you have while trying to get what you want. For example, let's say that you need more money. You're not broke, hungry, or homeless, but you are tired of living paycheck to paycheck. In your quest for more, you do some unethical, illegal, or even immoral things. You cheat on your taxes, lie about your income to qualify for a government program, steal from your employer.

While it feels like you're getting more, you have actually put yourself at risk for losing what you had to begin with. Yes, your house is small, but a prison cell is smaller. Sure, your spouse may meet only eighty percent of your needs, but would you rather be a divorced single parent with no partner at all? Fifty-thousand dollars a year may not go far, but it is better than being unemployed with a salary of zero.

My friend, I don't know who you are or when you may read this book. But, this section on taking nothing for granted was added when I thought that I was done writing this book. It is a powerful reminder that God wanted you to read. Take nothing for granted. Often, once you express gratitude for what you currently have, that is when God is able to bless you with more. Love and appreciate the people in your life, the place where God has you, and the things you have been blessed with. Love your life right where you are, okay?

## Prayer For Count Your Blessings

Father God, I thank you for what I have and for what I do not have. I thank you for my problems. Yes, my problems, because they are just a chance for you to come through with a solution or a miracle. I also thank you for the problems that I don't have. While things may be bad, they could be a whole lot worse.

Thank you for being the silver lining in all of my cloudy days. Forgive me for my complaining. Please help me to always count my blessings. In the name of Jesus, I pray. Amen.

## A Reflection

In this chapter, we discussed counting our blessings. Whenever we are stressed or upset, it can be hard to find something to be grateful for. Yet, gratitude is such an important trait to have. A good way to practice gratitude is to look at a person, a place, or thing and break down all of the blessings that made it possible. For example, when you come home to a dirty house and feel overwhelmed with housework, stop and take a minute to thank God for a home, for beds that you can sleep in, dishes that you can eat from. Thank Him for the garbage that is the result of being able to feed your family, etc. . . . you get the point. Use the space below to begin to write down your blessings. I suspect once you get started, you will run out of room to write!

_____

_____

_____

_____

_____

_____

_____

# Everything
## Comes Full Circle

"Yet what we suffer now is nothing compared to the glory he will reveal to us later."

—Romans 8:18 NLT

This Scripture is one that gives me life! My eldest son's birthday is August 18th. And of all of the books of the Bible that have the eighth chapter and an eighteenth verse, Romans 8:18 is the one that God gave me to speak over my oldest son's life. I'll share the details surrounding my son's birth in a few pages. First, I want to share a few other examples of suffering giving way to glory.

When we are going through a tough situation, it can truly seem as though God has forgotten all about us. It can also seem as God is having fun with your life. Growing up, I was fully convinced that God put me on this Earth and gave me this crappy life just so that other people could look at me and feel better about themselves. At around twelve years old or so, I couldn't wait until I died and could finally talk to God face to face — and ask Him, "Why?"

It was also around that time that I first experienced losing my hair. One day, while we were getting ready to go somewhere, I was combing my hair and noticed it was all over the table — I was sitting at the kitchen table. That's what you do when you are in a family of six and have only one bathroom and no dresser in your bedroom — my hair was literally shredding. Over time, the back of my head looked like someone had taken a dull razor to certain spots and used crooked scissors in other parts. Because, of course, when your hair sheds, it wouldn't dare fall out nice and evenly! The kids at school had a field day with my newfound hairdo. But, in addition to being teased at school, I also had to deal with my mother's theories about my hair loss.

My mom didn't take me to the doctor or the hairdresser. Yet, she came up with her own reasons why my hair was falling out. Her theories ranged from me simply cutting my hair in my spare time to my having cancer. The most hurtful and outlandish theory of them all was that I was a prostitute. Somehow, I was having enough sex (at the age of thirteen) to literally rub most of my hair off of my head. If you are hoping that I just made that up to make for a more exciting book, trust me, I wish I were making it up. Over the next few months, my hair grew back.

Unfortunately, I went through a few more cycles of hair loss and regrowth over the years. Now, as an adult, I am able to thwart it by paying careful attention to my hair — and by staying off the streets and having less sex (just kidding!).

Now that you know my hair loss story, you will understand the glory of this next account. In 2009 or 2010, the assistant principal at the high school where I worked called me into her office one day. When I got to her office, there was a female student sitting there. The female student was in the habit of wearing a hat or a bandana to school each day. She was in the office because wearing headgear of any type was against the school uniform policy. So, when the assistant principal told the young lady to remove her bandana, she refused to do it and began to cry.

She then explained her situation and showed the assistant principal her hair loss. She was embarrassed to walk around with her hair like that, but she didn't know what to do. Now, for some reason, the assistant principal got the idea that I, *Ann-Gela*, could help her (insert tears). When I arrived at her office, she told me the young woman's story. Then she said that, since I was such a diva and fashionista who is always so put together, I surely must have an extra wig at home for the student!

My response was, "I sure do. I'll bring you a wig first thing tomorrow morning. Okay, honey?"

The next day I brought her a wig. Actually, I brought her two wigs, two wig caps, a wig brush, a bottle of wig spray, and two Styrofoam heads to help keep their shape at night. This young woman was not going to have to walk around being depressed, self-conscious, and teased on my watch! When I gave everything to her, she cried. She cried and said to me, "Thank you, Miss! You have no idea how you just saved my life!"

I gave her a hug and told her to see me if she ever needed anything else. Then, I excused myself, went to the ladies' room, and cried.

## Glory revealed

Someone said that your misery is a clue to your ministry. Your pain points you to your purpose. The place of your greatest agony is where God gives you your greatest victories. Life often doesn't turn out the way we want it to. Remember, at the beginning of the chapter, when I asked if God was using my life to help other people feel better about theirs? What if that was true? Not in the way I thought, but through incidents like this one.

I thought people would look at my life, see the mess that it was in and thank God that they didn't have my life. Yet, what if folks are looking at my life and realize that they, too, can make it? Dear reader, this applies to you too! Where is your greatest pain? Let me encourage you that there is purpose in that! Someone else needs to hear how you overcame:

Abuse
Abandonment
Drug abuse
Alcoholism
Imprisonment
Teen pregnancy
Homelessness
Marriage failure
Business loss
Low self-esteem
Countless other issues, great and small

Even if you are still dealing with it at this present moment, even if you are still facing it, or even if you are still in the middle of it with no sight of actually overcoming this thing, be encouraged! What you are facing comes with lessons for you, and lessons for others. Your present suffering cannot compare to the glory that will be revealed!

## Prayer For Everything Comes Full Circle

Father God, I thank you that, even in the midst of the most difficult circumstances, I have hope. I not only have hope, but I have a promise. A promise that my present suffering cannot compare to the glory that will be revealed. When times are tough, please remind me to hold on and to keep looking towards you. If I continue in your will and follow the path that you have outlined for me, I will get through this. And one day, I will be on the other side of this. I'm excited about being on that side of things — the glory side — the side where I can share my testimony and offer help to someone else.

I thank you for not only getting me through this season, but also for building true compassion in me. Because of what I am going through and have been through, my compassion for others in this area is real! It is all for your glory! In the name of Jesus, I pray. Amen.

# A Reflection

In this chapter, we discussed everything coming full circle. Have you experienced this for yourself? Do you have an example like my hair example that demonstrated how God could use your pain? What about a current situation that you do not understand while you are going through it? Write the vision of how God may one day use your testimony to be a blessing to others! Write it with hope and expectancy!

_____

_____

_____

_____

_____

_____

_____

_____

_____

_____

_____

_____

_____

# TRUST THE PROCESS

*"Let all that I am wait quietly before God, for my hope is in him."*

—Psalm 62:5 NLT

T*he previous chapters of* this book were about the following lessons that I've learned:

Grace for the moment.
Timing is Everything!
Your first impression may be wrong.
Hold off on your good or bad judgment of a thing.
How I learned to overcome jealousy.
Find the lesson in everything.
Count your blessings.
Everything comes full circle.

This final chapter about trusting the process basically sums up all of those lessons in one. Although I first started to write this book in 2015, events that took place in 2016 made me realized all that I've learned and how it all came together.

In 2001, I was at a large outdoor concert in our city where Ray Charles was performing. It was estimated that over ten thousand people were in attendance. At one point in the evening, I happened to glance across the crowd, when the

Lord spoke to me. He told me that He would use me to speak to a crowd that size one day. Again, that was in 2001.

In 2016, some fifteen years later, I had the pleasure and honor of being the commencement speaker at the graduation of my former high school. It was nothing short of an honor! They could have asked a thousand other people: Former graduates, business owners, or educators. It turns out that I was their first choice. Little did the graduation committee know that I had been working on my speech for twenty-one years.

In 1996, when I was nineteen years old, I gave birth to my son. I had just finished my first year of college when I returned home for the summer to give birth. My first year of college had been paid for. In fact, all four years of my college education had been paid for because I had earned a full, four-year scholarship. I had been a straight-A student all throughout my school years. I was voted 'Most Likely to Succeed' and was named Valedictorian of my graduating class.

But, instead of utilizing that scholarship and getting my education, I found myself giving birth to a baby boy on the eleventh floor of Yale New Haven Children's Hospital. His dad eventually showed up to the hospital yet hadn't answered his phone or pages all day as I was in labor and looking for someone who could drive me to the hospital. Perhaps he was too busy. While I was just nineteen and had responsibilities as a college student, he was a thirty-year-old man with a job and a thriving drug-dealing business on the side. He wasn't the guy who stood on corners "nickel and diming it".

His drug deals usually netted him $1,000 or more in one transaction.

And before you judge me for dating a drug dealer, I had no clue that he sold drugs. He had a job. I actually met him at his job. He was a gas station attendant. Surely his legitimate job at the gas station was enough to pay for his Mustang and account for the wallet full of money. (Yes, you can laugh at my innocence or ignorance. Whatever you want to call it.)

He also had a family. He wasn't married. He lived with a woman with whom he had two children. Again, before you judge me for being his side chick, I didn't know. I didn't find out about this woman until she called the out-of-state phone number that kept showing up on her long-distance bill. When she called the number, the phone rang in my dorm room. We figured out who each of us was, and we even swapped pregnancy stories, since we were both pregnant by this man at the same time. Our kids, whom to this day have never met, were born a mere three months apart.

So, not only did I drop out of college and lose my full four-year scholarship, but I also learned that the man who I was in love with wasn't in love with me; he lived with a woman who was also carrying his baby. And I thought that my hair falling out at twelve was enough to make me want to die...

After my son was born, I spent the next few years in a deep state of depression. My old friends from college kept in touch with me. And while I was changing diapers, asking WIC for extra formula vouchers, and paying for cab rides to take my son to the doctor, they were pledging sororities and preparing for graduation. My son's dad came around every now and then. But, as far as a relationship was concerned, he flat out told me that he had other women to choose from, and I didn't rank very high on the list. He even ran his fingers through my hair and told me that he could never be with someone whose hair fell out like that. Again, this is not some embellishment on my part for a good story; this is all true — although I wish it was not.

After that, I was on a mission to find a man. My son needed a father, and for some reason, I believed that without a man, I was nothing, even though it was my relationship with a man that changed the course of my life and sent me into a downward spiral. Nevertheless, old habits are hard to break. So, I went from one relationship to the next, looking for healing that only came from God.

It shouldn't come as a surprise that I kept dating the same guy over and over. Sure, he had a different name and a different face, but trust me, it was the same guy.

During those years, my life teetered over the edge of insanity, but God never let me fall. I not only survived, but I thrived. I didn't realize just how much God had brought me through until I stepped up to the podium on that graduation stage.

## My Graduation Speech Was Entitled, "You Can Do It!"

In just under eight minutes — the maximum time

recommended for a speech according to Toastmasters International — I gave the crowd my life story. In eight minutes, I covered a span of twenty-one years. I summed up every tear, every lesson, every long walk home, every heartbreak, every disappointment. I was, at first, hesitant to tell my story because I would be revealing details of my personal life to people that I worked with, people whose lives had gone well and as planned. I knew that they would not be able to sympathize with me and would also probably judge me. However, I also knew what God had called me to do, so my hesitation didn't last long.

After I gave the speech, I received a standing ovation. That was nice. But, to be honest, what touched me the most was the young woman who ran up to greet me after graduation with tears in her eyes. She told me how she had felt like giving up, and how she now felt so much better after hearing my story! In eight minutes, God had used me to change the course of her life.

I was overwhelmed with the response from everyone. Especially from those people who I thought had perfect lives and couldn't possibly learn anything from me. That night, God showed me two things. One, although it had been fifteen years since that Ray Charles concert, that graduation only had about two thousand people in attendance. The big stage with over ten thousand people was still to come. Two, that speech that I gave in 2016 couldn't have been given in any prior year. I needed each and every experience up until that time to help write that speech. Not just the content, but the spirit of humbleness, the eagerness to really help someone, the surrender to God to tell my testimony, and not be afraid of their faces. It took all of that time to get it just right.

Life doesn't give us what we expect, and that's all we really should expect — that, and the fact that God's hand is always there. Your time is coming. Trust the process. Know that everything good, bad, and ugly is really working for your good. Your mistakes are lessons. Your rejections are God's redirection. Your enemies are the audience for your blessings. Your misfortunes are avenues to learn God's way and experience His hand of favor when you think you have nothing left.

I've told you what I know. I couldn't possibly begin to tell you what I don't know. Once I learn it, I will write another book. *God bless you!*

## Prayer For Trust The Process

Father God, in the name of Jesus. Whew! Life can be quite a journey. There are things I want. Things I don't want. I have experienced things that I could not have imagined, both good and bad. Yet, I am still here. While I have breath, I have hope! My hope isn't for life to get easier for me to finally get everything that I want. No, my hope is that I will continue to see the goodness of the Lord in the land of the living. Life is a precious, precious gift. I want to repeat that. Life is a precious, precious gift! My ability to navigate this life is directly proportional to your presence in my life. I cannot do this without you. I do not want to do this without you. Not now and certainly not for eternity.

I thank you, Father, for the sacrifice of Jesus' blood on the cross. I thank you that He died for my sins. Without the shedding of blood, there can be no remission of sins. I believe in my heart and confess with my mouth, the Lord Jesus. Through His death, I have access to the Throne of Grace to receive mercy and help. I belong to you, Lord.

Help me to live my best life, full of purpose and promise. In the name of Jesus, I pray. Amen.

## A Reflection

Throughout this book, we have focused on trusting the process. We do not know everything. Everything is not as bad as it seems. There are things we will be uncertain about. And there are questions that we may wait a long time to receive the answer to, or we may never get the answer at all. That is life. Still, God is on the throne and in control! He knew everything we would face. He sent His only begotten son to walk in our place. Not only in day-to-day life, but even in death, He took our place. Do you believe that? Would you like to accept Jesus Christ as your Savior?

In this section, write down what you have discovered about God, yourself, and your wonderful life. If you feel lead to do so, email me your final reflection. It will be kept with the highest confidentiality. I would love to know that God has blessed you through this book. And if not, feel free to let me know that too. Criticism, like everything else, is just a part of life. Be Blessed!

_____

_____

_____

_____

_____

_____

_____

_____

_____

_____

_____

_____

_____

_____

_____

_____

# About The Author

Ann-Gela Holloway was born in New Haven, Connecticut. Number four in a family of five, and the oldest daughter. Her father named her and came up with the unique spelling; a name that she did not like while growing up because it did not seem special enough.

She is the proud mother of two sons, Andre and Alexander. Her sons have an almost sixteen-year age difference. Because of that, they both were each raised as an only child.

In addition to writing books, Ann-Gela also writes poetry and blogs. She performs as an actress and a spoken word artist. She hosts a podcast entitled *Chit-Chat: It's more than just talk.*

She gives back by volunteering as a Sunday School teacher for the past twelve years. She also runs workshops for students to help them with job applications, college essays, resume writing, and how to dress for success.

Ann-Gela earned her bachelor's degree in Business Management from Albertus Magnus College in New Haven, CT. She is nine credits shy of obtaining her master's degree in Business Administration. She has been employed by the State of Connecticut since 2003. In 2019, she launched Ann-Gela Holloway Consulting. Her business specializes in resume writing, job coaching, and life coaching.